Farewell, My Dudes

D0925896

69 Dystopian Haikus

Johnathan Rice

Farewell, My Dudes:
69 Dystopian Haikus

Johnathan Rice

HAT & BEARD | LOS ANGELES

Farewell, My Dudes: 69 Dystopian Haikus

First North American Edition
Copyright © 2017 by Hat & Beard Press

ISBN: 978-0-9987239-3-8

Edited by Jessica Hundley
Essay by Mandy Kahn
Art Direction by Brian Roettinger
Designed by Taylor Giali
Production by Lisa Bechtold
Copy Editing by Lara Schoorl, Christie Hayden, and Sybil Perez

Printed by GLS Companies in St. Paul, Minnesota

Hat & Beard Press
2438½ N. Beachwood Dr.
Los Angeles, CA 90068

www.hatandbeard.com

Contents

61	Vapid Performance Fabrication
63	Crystal Feathers Spa on the Go, LLC.
65	City of Loneliness
67	San Pedro, California, Suckin City
69	Love Sad
71	Camp No Friends
73	Desperation Lake
75	Human Extinction Now
77	Guacamole Inn
79	Little Armageddon
81	Annoying Health Centre
83	Trump Dog Beach
85	Climate of Change
87	Fleetwood Macchiato
89	Cool Character Costume & Party Hire
91	No Anxiety Crew
93	Self Righteous
95	Hedonist Artisan Ice Cream
97	The Antisocial Butterfly
99	Food Styling by Jess
101	Beyond Abandoned
103	Death Squad
105	Paranormal Friends UK
107	Milk and Honey Birth
109	Get It While You Can
111	Make Cookies Great Again
113	Vengeance University
115	Tripple A Porto-Potties
117	Suspicious Garage
119	Agony of Da Feet

Twenty-Two Thoughts After Reading Haikus by Johnathan Rice

Mandy Kahn

1. Poetry's brevity makes it an ideal form for our time.
2. Poetry can be timely.
3. Poems can be funny. They can even be hilarious.
4. Social media is a very efficient means of delivering poems.
5. The Japanese haikuist known as Issa, an eighteenth-century Buddhist priest, was often funny, too:

Don't worry, spiders,
I keep house
casually.

Climb Mount Fuji,
O snail,
but slowly, slowly.

Issa is a pen name; it means "cup of tea."

Thoughts of how tea's leaves
are dried, then boiled, how each
leaf contains the plant—how each
cup contains the field.*

6. There are as many ways of
making a life in poetry as there are
poets living.

7. Strict poetic forms can be
adapted, reinvented. Their rules
can make good kindling for new
ideas of form.

8. Poetry and music both have
roots in the bardic tradition.
What's remarkable is that we've
separated them.
    The Homeric poems were
performed with an accompaniment
on lyre. Some scholars claim that
they were sung.

9. To cultivate new readers, share
poems in new ways. We must meet
readers where they read.

10. There are already new audiences
for poetry. They're already being
cultivated.

11. Poetry, when encountered
unexpectedly, can be unexpectedly loved. One might love it
accidentally.

*Issa's poems appear in a translation by Robert Hass.

12. Comedy, too, has roots in the bardic tradition.
13. The power of a regular creative practice is that it builds a lens for us; it invites us to look carefully, but pointedly. The musician looks for the song; the screenwriter looks for the story; the poet looks— and waits—for the arrival of the poem.

    The poet who works diligently is available when the poem arrives. OR: The song, the story, the poem is perpetually stepping forward; she who's engaged in the practice of making perpetually is watching for it and notices.
14. An idea stated briefly—or an image—can be easily shared and recalled.
15. Poetry can feel light. Reading it can feel effortless.
16. Poetry shared immediately can participate in the discussions of its day.
17. Poetry can have teeth.
18. This is a lucky moment to be alive and making work. We have a free means of dissemination, and

printing costs are less than they've ever been; when bought by the ream, paper's a penny a page. (Thoughts of Emily Dickinson writing poems on the inside flaps of envelopes she'd gotten in the mail, because of thrift.)

19.   It's been said that comedy is tragedy plus time. Perhaps it's tragedy plus form.

20.   Thoughts of Kerouac's very funny haiku. Here are two:

I went into the woods
to meditate—
it was too cold

Bee, why are you
staring at me?
I'm not a flower!

21.   Perhaps sharing work very quickly means a person's fear of sharing it is lessened. Maybe it does not.

22.   Poetry is dynamic. It will find a way to navigate new systems; it will forge new ways through us.

Small Time Criminals

We can't break the law
But squirrels break it daily
And they are naked

Exorcist

Your ex likes your pics
Cuz she wants you to suffer
And go slowly mad

Trump America

All sexy ladies
Will report to the dance floor
For deportation

Avoiding the Real World

Your problems just called
They know where you are going
And they'll meet you there

Creepypasta Paranormal Vn

Towel dispenser
Did not blink, gave no towel
He knew he was dead

Politically Inconsiderate Pies

Today was so great
 Until I happened to see
The way that you parked

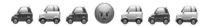

Owning Our Ignorance

Bae told me a lie
It was the lie that baes tell
"I'm not that hungry"

Small Balls and Larry

She said "NBD"
He was totes relieved, because
His D's not that big

U Flaky

Come visit L.A.
But please call ahead, darling
So I can split town

Beard of God

We cannot defeat
These entitled baristas
They have the coffee

Sociopathic Apps

I know that you talk
About me in therapy
Because I'm outside

Crotch Rockets

Your sweet old father
Saw your Coachella outfit
And wept in his car

Sweet & Woodsy Aromatherapy

You are in the woods
To find peace and privacy
You took hella pics

Pretentious Pet Portraits

Nice to meet you, Hawk
I was there the night your Mom
Got high and named you

Pretty Horrible Faces

I don't want to know
Anything about your cat
Or see its picture

Boho Vibes

We can't all wear hats
So I will go without one
To balance the vibe

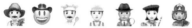

The Paleo Kingdom

Brother Fred Flintstone
You were truly paleo
Mad respect, my dude

Little Dudes Only

When I say "my dudes"
It's not a possessive vibe
It's friendly, my dudes

We Are Curated

Aesthetically
There's no fucking way that this
Will ever work out

Weiner & Weiner

What is a snake, bro?
It's a dangerous noodle
That bites IRL

Vapid Performance Fabrication

Ur snapchat story
An unwitting document
Of a hollow life

Crystal Feathers Spa on the Go, LLC.

Is your job really
Taking pictures of feathers?
That fills me with rage

City of Loneliness

Her sexy pictures
Help her to briefly forget
Her father left her

San Pedro, California, Suckin City

Music is free now
But the joke is on us, dudes
'Cause most of it sucks

Love Sad

There is no cure for Love
 But by the end of the year
There will be like five

Camp No Friends

Let's meet up later
And if you flake out again
I'll see you in Hell

Desperation Lake

She won't text me back
But she shares pics of her lunch
With the whole wide world

Human Extinction Now

Intellectuals
Who warned us of extinction
Will soon be extinct

Guacamole Inn

I just heard about
Your guacamole podcast
And became angry

Little Armageddon

The foretold Rapture
 Is happening tomorrow
You're not on the list

Annoying Health Centre

Everything he had
He put into his smoothie
It was not enough

Trump Dog Beach

We are witnesses
To America's decline
And it's ducking lit

Climate of Change

The future looks bright
 But that is mostly because
 It will be on fire

Fleetwood Macchiato

Without Stevie Nicks
There would be no Tumblr, dudes
Just chicks wearing hats

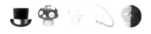

Cool Character Costume & Party Hire

His hip vintage threads
Belie his mortal terror
For the here and now

  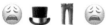

No Anxiety Crew

The power of our
 Sharp collective anxiety
 Could light the world, Fam

Self Righteous

Saw you took a break
From all social media
Cuz you posted it

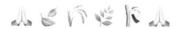

Hedonist Artisan Ice Cream

I respect your vibe
Emotionally threadbare
But still down to rage

The Antisocial Butterfly

I had a nightmare
I was walking down the street
Everyone said "hi"

Food Styling by Jess

You can bet your ass
There won't be room on the Arc
For the food stylists

Beyond Abandoned

"I'm catching feelings"
She said, as she fell asleep
He left before dawn

Death Squad

Celebs have worked hard
At redefining squad goals
Friendship now means less

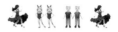

Paranormal Friends UK

There's a ghost in here
But that is totes chill with me
Now I'm not alone

Milk and Honey Birth

The party was weird
Because, my dudes, it was a
Placenta party

Get It While You Can

She gave him the eye
At the very same weird bar
He raged with her dad

Make Cookies Great Again

Grandma made cookies
Sadly, Grandma is also
Totally racist

Vengeance University

Old Tinder matches
Are at the Glendale Whole Foods
Plotting your demise

Tripple A Porto-Potties

Dear Mr. DJ
I know you played Marquee Moon
'Cuz you have to pee

Suspicious Garage

You're so vain, BB
You think this ku's about you
In this case you're right

Agony of Da Feet

Who would have known that
My tears, shame, and fear would make
This flavorful broth

Duck Commander

World War Three, my dudes
Will very likely be caused
By autocorrect

    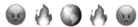

Please Stop

If you're prolific
But most of your shit is wack
You're punishing us

Final Bridge of Insecurity

Losing followers
Never bothered the Jesus
But it bothers me

Redeemer Lutheran Church

When so moved, send nudes
But beware, ye lustful thots
They might get sent back

Charlatan Tower

Your aura is blue?
That comes as a wee surprise
I thought it was gnar

FAKE NEWS

Truth may be dying
But you're not a real model
And we all know it

No Filter No Glory

The filter you used
The nose and ears of a dog
You look like a bitch

Everything is a GIF

Many fine people
Who throw down a real chill vibe
Are on klonopin

Project Brunch

She was totes well read
And her fave music era?
Pre-moustache Misty

Bohemian Baby Booty

Hello, I'm the guy
Who gets high with your parents
While you are asleep

Focus on Malnutrition

Vegans love cookies
Cuz cookies are totes delish
And cuz they're starving

Vintage ROCK

If you play The Weight
With your band at your concert
'Twill be our last waltz

Pretentious Headquarters

Esoteric posts
Are risks she's willing to take
Cuz she's an Aries

Nuclear Family

Tonight, her two Dads
Were fighting with her three Moms
So dinner was weird

Passive Aggressive Designs, INC.

"I'm down for whatevs"
Is what she says to me now
Lying through perfect teeth

Walls To Build Bridges

Your black sombrero
Is truly freaking me out
Because I'm shrooming

Lothario Lounge

"What do you do, sir?"
"I vibe out, make dank haiku"
-her blouse falls right off-

Crazy Buffet

She said she was bi
But neglected to mention
She meant bipolar

Whatever

Sorry you found out
We went for drinks after
Your intervention

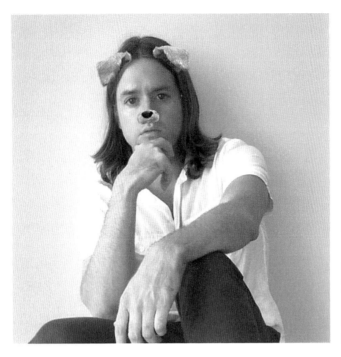

Johnathan Rice was signed to Reprise Records in 2003 and has been writing, recording, and producing music ever since. He spent his twenties touring the world and disgracing his family's good name. More recently he has sought to add insult to injury and now finds himself in Hollywood, where the nexus of music and film meet. In *Farewell, My Dudes*, his debut book of poetry, Rice uses humor and haiku to comment on what he feels may be a disintegrating culture, and his own complicity in it.